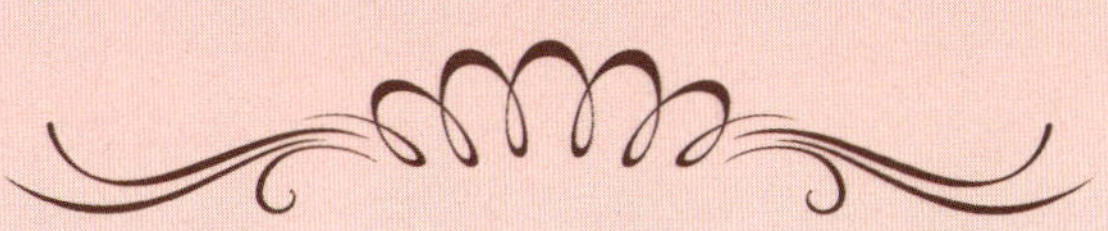

COLORING BUTTERFLIES

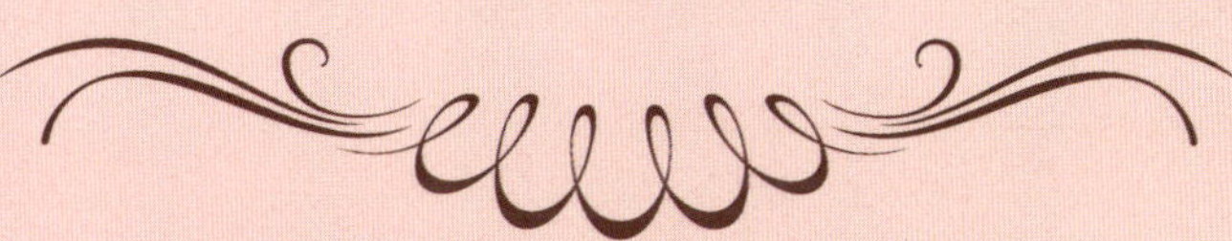

OVER 40 DELIGHTFUL
PICTURES WITH FULL
COLORING GUIDES

ARCTURUS

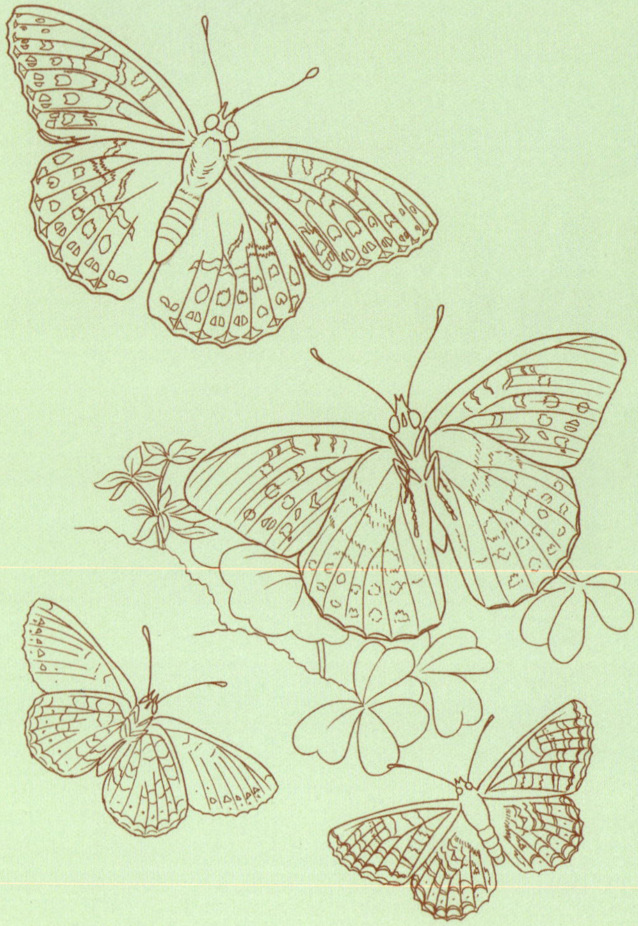

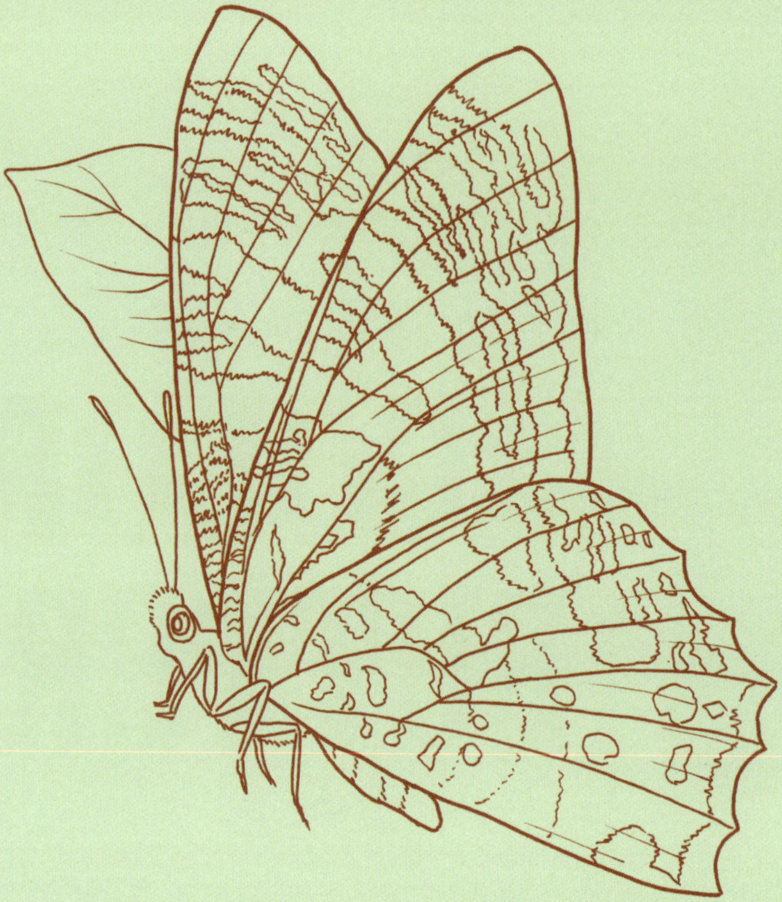

This edition published in 2016 by Arcturus Publishing Limited
26/27 Bickels Yard, 151–153 Bermondsey Street,
London SE1 3HA

ISBN: 978-1-78599-243-8
CH004983US
Supplier 26, Date 0116, Print Run 4892

Printed in China

Introduction

Artists have been attracted to butterflies for centuries–in fact they even appear among prehistoric Pyrenean cave paintings and on Minoan artefacts from 4,000 years ago. It wasn't just their beauty that made them important in the ancient world, for they were also regarded as spirits and in ancient Greece they were linked to the human soul.

Many artists and naturalists over the years have devoted time to making beautiful, painstaking depictions of the intricate markings and jeweled colors of butterfly wings. The plates in this book come from *The Naturalist's Library*, which was edited by the great Scottish naturalist Sir William Jardine (1800-1874) and issued in a set of 40 volumes with more than 1,300 engraved plates. Exquisitely rendered, the butterflies are shown in their natural habitat, set against the flora where you might expect to find them in the wild. The illustrations were engraved by William Lizars (1788-1859).

It would be impossible to paint a butterfly in detail from life, since they come to rest only briefly. This makes them an ideal subject for a coloring book, where time is unlimited to study their patterns and colorations. There was a time when coloring in was regarded as something strictly for children, but today adults too have discovered the enjoyment of this form of art, where all the attention is devoted to color without worrying about getting a drawing right first. We know now, too, how relaxing it is for the mind to be focused on one absorbing activity, shutting out the stresses of life.

The choice of art materials is now very wide, and you can work with oil-based, wax-based or watersoluble color pencils–an easy way to start. You can use them dry, blending them with your finger or a paper stump, or dilute them with oil, or water for the watersoluble pencils. Should you wish to paint, a small watercolor set and a medium-sized round brush is all you need. Whichever you choose, you'll find huge enjoyment from coloring in these beautiful butterflies.

Diana Vowles

Key: *List of plates*

1 1 & 2 *Pieris epicharis*
3 *P. philyra*

2 1 *Leptocircus curius*
2 *Thais medesicaste*

3 1 *Papilio protesilaus*
2 *P. sinon*

4 1 *Marius thetis*
2 *Fabius hippona*

5 1 & 2 *Polyommatus venus*
3 & 4 *P. achaeus*

6 *Thaliura rhipheus*

7 1 *Argynnis adippe*
2 *A. lathonia*

8 1 & 2 *Polyommatus Marsyas*
3 & 4 *P. endymion*

9 *Rhipheus dasycephalus*

10 1 *Deiopeia bella*
2 *Cydosia nobilitella*
3 *Chloridea rhexiae*
4 *Alaria gaurae*
5 *Caterpillar*

11 1 *Gonepteryx rhamni*
2 *Colias edusa*

12 1 & 2 *Helicopis gnidus*
3 *Erycina octavius*

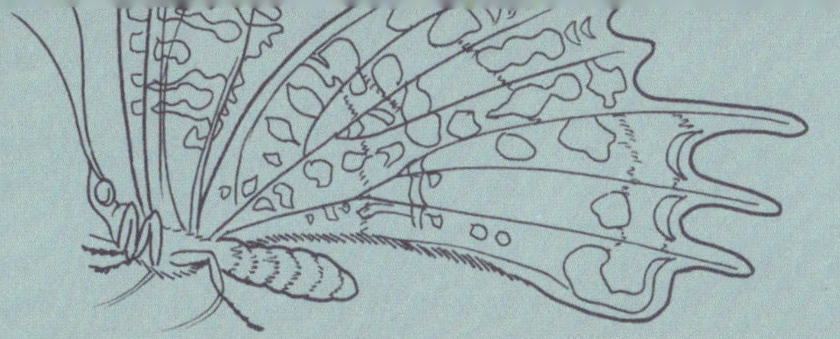

13 1 *Nymphalis ethiocles*
2 & 3 *N. tiridates*

14 1 *Peridromia arethusa*
2 *P. amphinome*

15 1 *Heleona fenestrata*
2 *Anthomyza teresia*

16 1 *Colias hyale*
2 *C. europome*

17 *Cethosia cyane*

18 1 *Heliconia erato*
2 *H. cynisca*
3 *H. sylvana*

19 1 *Melitaea athalia, var.*
2 *M. artemis*
3 *M. silene*

20 1 *Papilio ascanius*
2 *P. paris*

21 1 & 2 *Heliconia flora*
3 *H. diaphana*
4 *Acraea pasiphae*

22 1 *Argynnis paphia*
2 *Melitaea cinxia*

23 *Charaxes jasius*

24 1 & 2 *Limacodes micilia*
3, 4, 5 *Doratifera vulnerans*

25 1 *Euploea limniace*
2 *E. plexippe*

26 *Hipparchia semele*
1 *Male* 2 *Female*
3 *H. megara*

27 1 *Callidryas eubule with caterpillar & chrysalis*
4 *Terias mexicana*

28 1 *Lycaena chryseis*
2 *L. hippothoe*
3 *L. phlaeas*

29 1 *Pieris belisama*
2 *Anthocharis danai*
3 *Iphias leucippe*

30 1 *Saturnia cynthia*
2 *S. mylitta*

31 1 *Polyommatus argiolus Male* 2 *Female*
3 *P. alsus* 4 *P. acis*

32 1 *Vanessa atalanta*
2 *Limenitis camilla*

33 1 *Papilio machaon*
2 *P. podalirius*

34 1 & 2 *Catochala neogama*
3 *C. amesia*

35 1 *Urania sloanus*
2 *U. leilus*

36 1 *Polyommatus arion*
2 *P. alcon*
3 *P. corydon*

37 *Cethosia dido*

38 *Caterpillars*

39 1 *Angerona prunaria*
2 *Alcis scolopacea*

40 1 *Agarista picta*
2 *Eusemia lectrix*
3 *E. maculatrix*

41 1 *Vanessa urtica*
2 *Cynthia cardia*

42 1 & 2 *Catagrama condomanus*
3 & 4 *C. pyramus*

43 1 *Nemeobius lucina*
2 *Melitaea athalia*

44 *Saturnia isis*

1 & 2 *Pieris epicharis* • 3 *P. philyra*

1 & 2 *Pieris epicharis* • 3 *P. philyra*

1 *Leptocircus curius* • 2 *Thais medesicaste*

1 *Leptocircus curius* • 2 *Thais medesicaste*

1 *Papilio protesilaus* • 2 *P. sinon*

1 *Papilio protesilaus* • 2 *P. sinon*

1 *Marius thetis* • 2 *Fabius hippona*

1 *Marius thetis* • 2 *Fabius hippona*

1 & 2 *Polyommatus venus* • 3 & 4 *P. achaeus*

1 & 2 *Polyommatus venus* • 3 & 4 *P. achaeus*

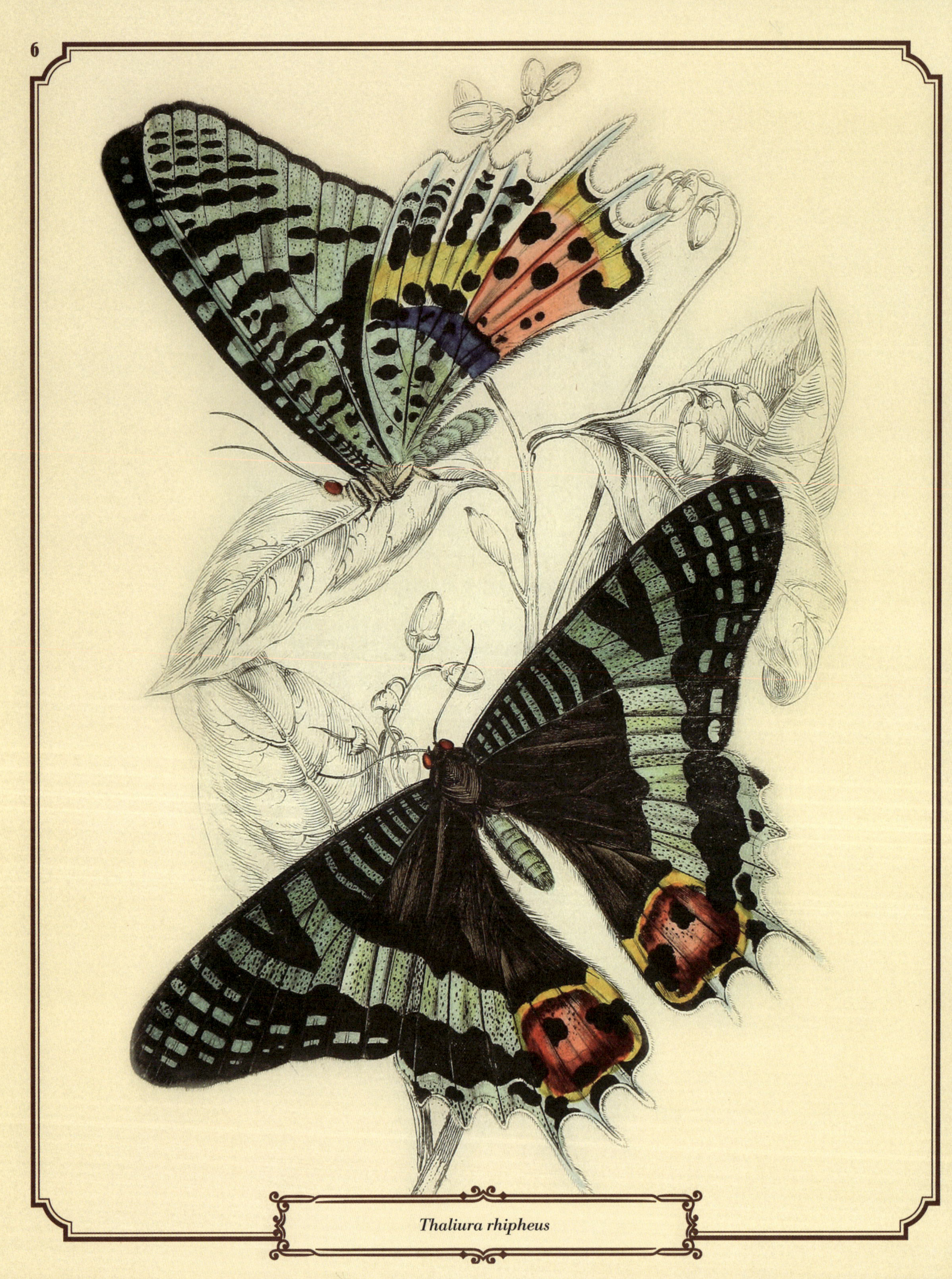

Thaliura rhipheus

Thaliura rhipheus

1 *Argynnis adippe* • 2 *A. lathonia*

1 *Argynnis adippe* • 2 *A. lathonia*

1 & 2 *Polyommatus Marsyas* • 3 & 4 *P. endymion*

1 & 2 *Polyommatus Marsyas* • 3 & 4 *P. endymion*

Rhipheus dasycephalus

Rhipheus dasycephalus

1 *Deiopeia bella* • 2 *Cydosia nobilitella*
3 *Chloridea rhexiae* • 4 *Alaria gaurae* • 5 *Caterpillar*

1 *Deiopeia bella* • 2 *Cydosia nobilitella*
3 *Chloridea rhexiae* • 4 *Alaria gaurae* • 5 *Caterpillar*

1 *Gonepteryx rhamni* • 2 *Colias edusa*

1 *Gonepteryx rhamni* • 2 *Colias edusa*

1 & 2 *Helicopis gnidus* • 3 *Erycina octavius*

1 & 2 *Helicopis gnidus* • 3 *Erycina octavius*

1 *Nymphalis ethiocles* • 2 & 3 *N. tiridates*

1 *Nymphalis ethiocles* • 2 & 3 *N. tiridates*

1 *Peridromia arethusa* • 2 *P. amphinome*

1 *Peridromia arethusa* • 2 *P. amphinome*

1 *Heleona fenestrata* • 2 *Anthomyza teresia*

1 *Heleona fenestrata* • 2 *Anthomyza teresia*

1 *Colias hyale* • 2 *C. europome*

1 *Colias hyale* • 2 *C. europome*

Cethosia cyane

Cethosia cyane

1 *Heliconia erato* • 2 *H. cynisca* • 3 *H. sylvana*

1 *Heliconia erato* • 2 *H. cynisca* • 3 *H. sylvana*

1 *Melitaea athalia, var.*
2 *M. artemis* • 3 *M. silene*

1 *Melitaea athalia, var.*
2 *M. artemis* • 3 *M. silene*

1 *Papilio ascanius* • 2 *P. paris*

1 *Papilio ascanius* • 2 *P. paris*

1 & 2 *Heliconia flora*
3 *H. diaphana* • 4 *Acraea pasiphae*

1 & 2 *Heliconia flora*
3 *H. diaphana* • 4 *Acraea pasiphae*

1 *Argynnis paphia* • 2 *Melitaea cinxia*

1 *Argynnis paphia* • 2 *Melitaea cinxia*

Charaxes jasius

Charaxes jasius

1 & 2 *Limacodes micilia*
3, 4, 5 *Doratifera vulnerans*

1 & 2 *Limacodes micilia*
3, 4, 5 *Doratifera vulnerans*

1 *Euploea limniace* • 2 *E. plexippe*

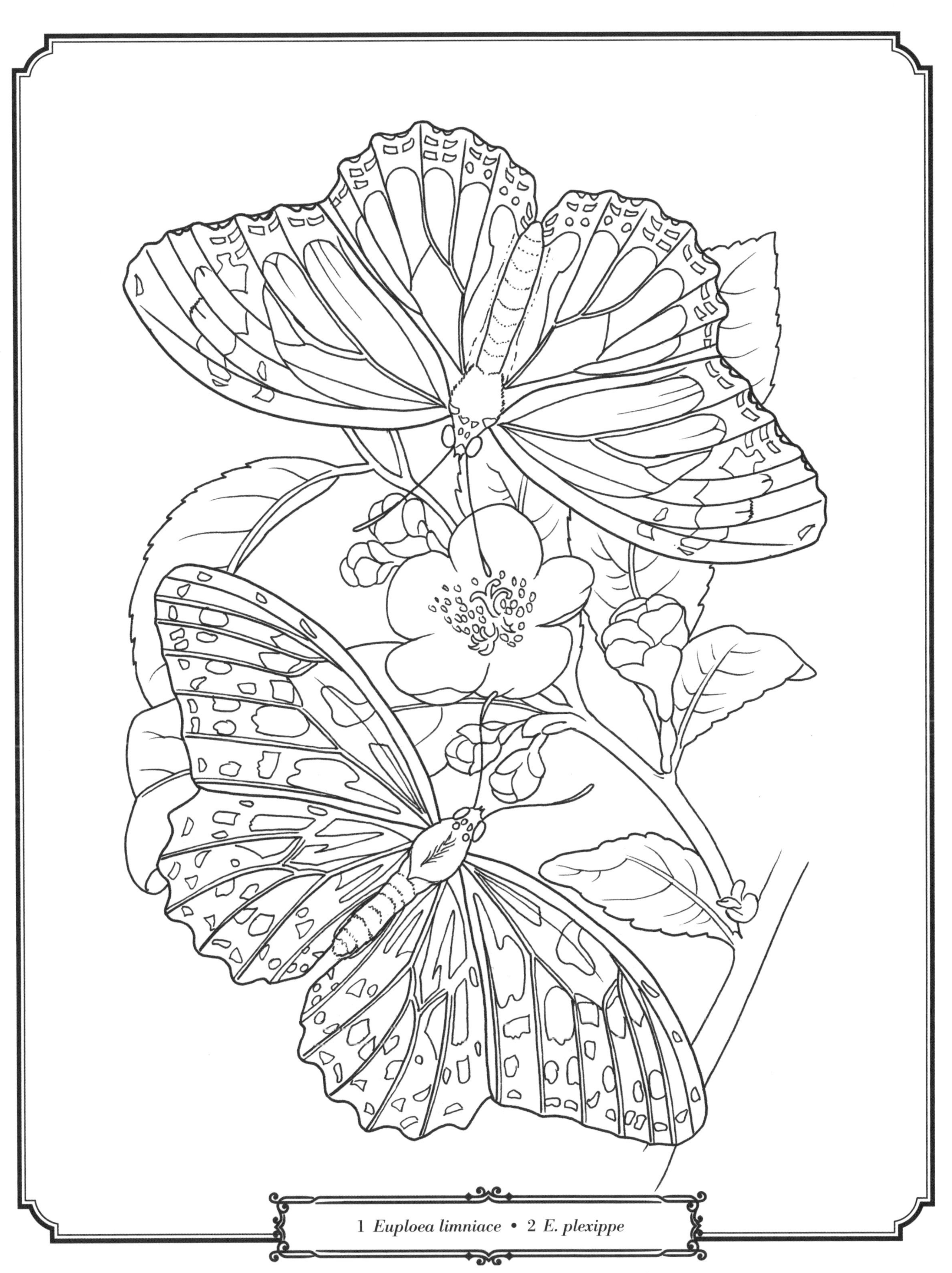

1 *Euploea limniace* • 2 *E. plexippe*

Hipparchia semele • 1 *Male*
2 *Female* • 3 *H. megara*

Hipparchia semele • 1 *Male*
2 *Female* • 3 *H. megara*

1 *Callidryas eubule with caterpillar & chrysalis*
4 *Terias mexicana*

1 *Callidryas eubule with caterpillar & chrysalis*
4 *Terias mexicana*

1 *Lycaena chryseis*
2 *L. hippothoe* • 3 *L. phlaeas*

1 *Lycaena chryseis*
2 *L. hippothoe* • 3 *L. phlaeas*

1 *Pieris belisama* • 2 *Anthocharis danai*
3 *Iphias leucippe*

1 *Pieris belisama* • 2 *Anthocharis danai*
3 *Iphias leucippe*

1 *Saturnia cynthia* • 2 *S. mylitta*

1 *Saturnia cynthia* • 2 *S. mylitta*

1 *Polyommatus argiolus Male* • 2 *Female*
3 *P. alsus* • 4 *P. acis*

1 *Polyommatus argiolus Male* • 2 *Female*
3 *P. alsus* • 4 *P. acis*

1 *Vanessa atalanta* • 2 *Limenitis camilla*

1 *Vanessa atalanta* • 2 *Limenitis camilla*

1 *Papilio machaon* • 2 *P. podalirius*

1 *Papilio machaon* • 2 *P. podalirius*

1 & 2 *Catochala neogama* • 3 *C. amesia*

1 & 2 *Catochala neogama* • 3 *C. amesia*

1 *Urania sloanus* • 2 *U. leilus*

1 *Urania sloanus* • 2 *U. leilus*

1 *Polyommatus arion* • 2 *P. alcon* • 3 *P. corydon*

1 *Polyommatus arion* • 2 *P. alcon* • 3 *P. corydon*

Cethosia dido

Cethosia dido

Caterpillars

Caterpillars

1 *Angerona prunaria* • 2 *Alcis scolopacea*

1 *Angerona prunaria* • 2 *Alcis scolopacea*

1 *Agarista picta*
2 *Eusemia lectrix* • 3 *E. maculatrix*

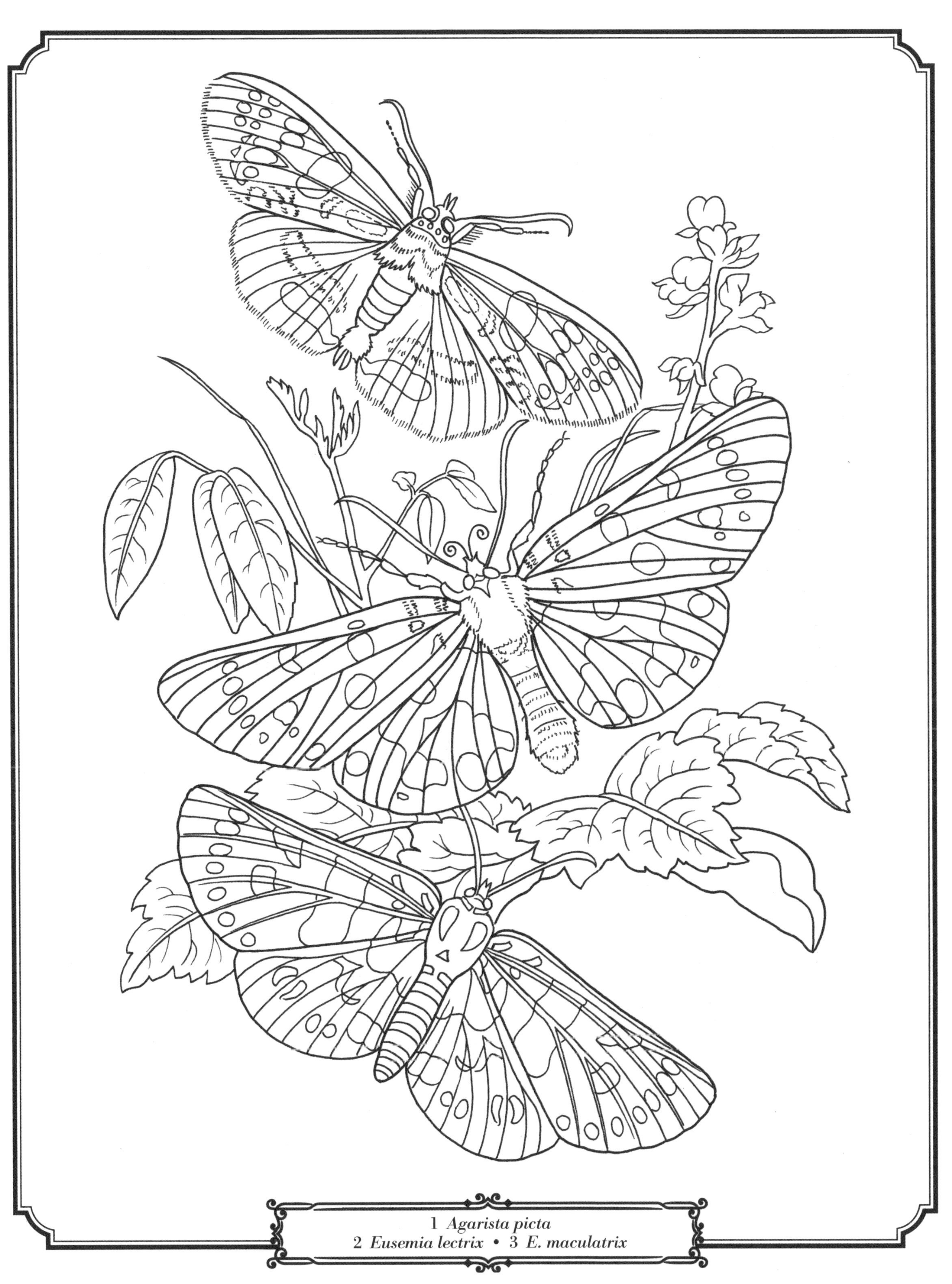

1 *Agarista picta*
2 *Eusemia lectrix* • 3 *E. maculatrix*

1 *Vanessa urtica* • 2 *Cynthia cardia*

1 *Vanessa urtica* • 2 *Cynthia cardia*

1 & 2 *Catagrama condomanus* • 3 & 4 *C. pyramus*

1 & 2 *Catagrama condomanus* • 3 & 4 *C. pyramus*

1 *Nemeobius lucina* • 2 *Melitaea athalia*

1 *Nemeobius lucina* • 2 *Melitaea athalia*

Saturnia isis

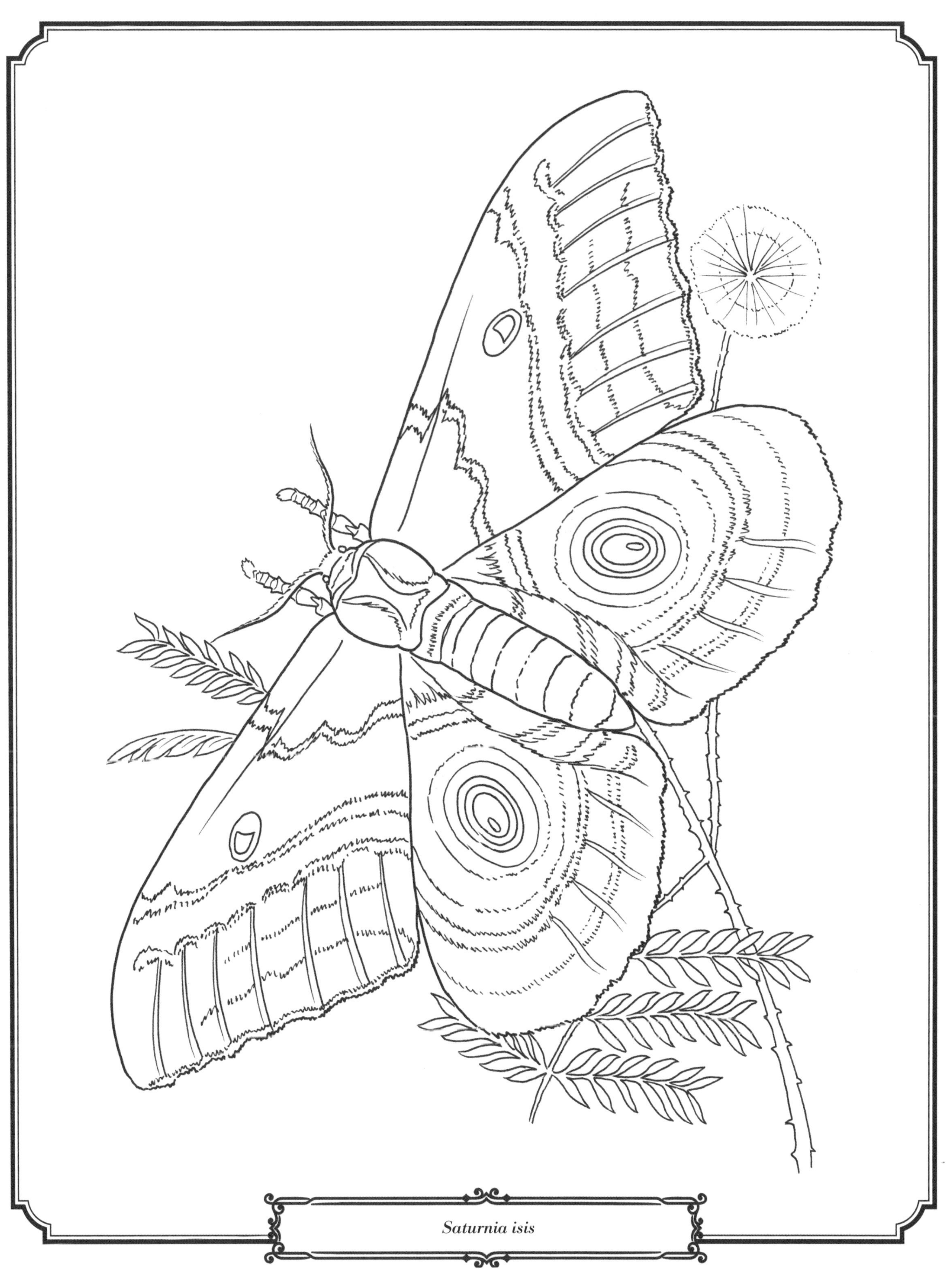
Saturnia isis